with
snow
pouring
southward
past
the
window

pitt

poetry

series

nancy krygowski

and

jeffrey mcdaniel

series editors

with snow pouring southward past the window

joan naviyuk kane

university of pittsburgh press

Published by the University of Pittsburgh Press, Pittsburgh, Pa., 15260

Manufactured in the United States of America
Printed on acid-free paper
10 9 8 7 6 5 4 3 2 1

ISBN 13: 978-0-8229-6766-8
ISBN 10: 0-8229-6766-9

Cover art © Tulluk, *Kubulujuu*, 2024. Pen on paper.

Cover and book design by Alex Wolfe

Publisher: University of Pittsburgh Press, 7500 Thomas Blvd., 4th floor, Pittsburgh, PA 15260, United States, www.upittpress.org

EU Authorized Representative: Easy Access System Europe, Mustamäe tee 50, 10621 Tallinn, Estonia, gpsr.requests@easproject.com

Contents

with
snow
pouring
southward
past
the
window

Trail Coltsfoot

our guttering winter's
    final blizzard
dizzies   bluebright
    pouring southward
        beyond the gold language
of the sun as it does not set
    & silvering women
    round the thaw
& glint like tin
    of Báhpajávri
where herons
    corvids gulls
        & four loons
    quorum   chasing light
                an arctic tern
            turns shriek
        to ternery
    & pearling nevernight
            strikes coltsfoot
        forth from marled soil
    & plitched
        hysteranthous is strewn
    into a line to track
as a woman crossing fjordward
    through the graves
palms these wilting
        capitulum

into the pockets
of her frock
& fools them
into a book
to transverse
the waters
churning blue-black
wavous
with calved floe & berg
as her blood
now courses
with blood & brain
of reindeer
changed to batter
& poured
onto a hot skillet
& tossed coinlike
& quartered by another
mother's dagger
& filled with lady's
mantle & chives & dandelions'
leaves & petalshut heads
& angelica umbels
& fireweed shoots & fresh
fen nettle tips

& smoked char & salmon
splits through bread
& ptarmigan
breast atop
a soup
of ptarmigan
stomach emptied
of the earliest
greenleaved willow
& reindeer
legs
braised in broth
& heaped
with last year's
redcurrant

& the lactated
cream
of the taxed
herd
now swum
in cloudberry
& then a tea
seeps
in snowmelt
of the torn blueberry
branches

& their campaniform

antheses

—may we ply the

time trailing

coltsfoot—

as loss trails

the last bloom

of the light as we leave her

with such women leafing through us

After Anchorage

Told to put a light in my lamp
I turned from a daughter's work
to take a tabular rock in hand
then struck as hail would strike,
as a man who has grown sick
of his wife will scrape and grind
as if he no longer hells infants
world-ward in their blood-rush,
hollowing a cup to hold the oil
I would otherwise have swallowed:
I trust in nothing near, hungering
for the light of the leaf as it unfurls,
tending what I can, beguiling none.
I tangled my neck in tresses, cutting
the necks from my dresses, snarling
what I knew, what I know I learned
down through my dirt floor. I could
have burned the smear of bear tallow
I once felt forced to eat on an arm
of the sea whose waves but wrought
their white across and up into wind
when what should harbor winter
now darkens down to parch.

Portland, January 1, 2025

. . . each out to catch an Indian for himself—
those maddening little women who kept calling . . .
—Elizabeth Bishop, "BRAZIL, JANUARY 1, 1502"

Januaries, Nature follies our senses
somewhat
as she
gritted theirs
with firework—

dread of the smoke
-loud dark
and how
it would reek
of greed

to rise with the
slow poem
of the new
year, with a voice
I mistook

for a grave
I wanted
to walk into: .
.
.

Now I
know like a willow
grove
like a kelp
grove

like a birch grove, a
spruce grove
like
angelica
in the hemlock

where the paperbark
boats should spin
away
on the wind
after fire,

wallowing after flood
after the ash
grave
and under such
ashpaper

as I called
to my mother
and never
having reached her
reaching, always

. . . calling to each other (or had the birds waked up?)
and retreating, always retreating, behind it . . .

After Anchorage I

had read the ash, the scoria: their slippage. There
rose no world, there
rises only islands.

So then we went away into the east to wait
until the stars began disappearing,
when at last we could ignore the natter

of what, during the last drought
proved to scare the calves we heard
only as noise as through heat
through the door on a train.

A refusal last time I slept
to dream of death.

Instead, I dreamt of trammeling
pasqueflower, of having swam
backward across the lake.

Don't Run Out

real & white as snow
have they forgotten
starting over & over

the swans crossing
with the dark tide
southward to the sound

not too far off
the firework & blast
of something hard to reach

& harder to escape

she remembers how
without him
a woman's quarrel

it passes into a quarrel
with no one

Din

Consounded in other ways I
grow fluent. One, distant, writes:

You   in my dream
conjuring fire
from some kind of spirits.

Years have passed, & again my mother asks
why I station a burnt sprit on the ledge.

Another, lost to me now on another ocean:

I had a dream about you last night.
We were on an island shore
watching icebergs drift by.

I will look through a darkness I could have walked through alone.

Letters from Learned Men

"Inupiaq words for 'dog' also have a special geographical distribution, since most dialects from North Alaskan Inupiaq east use some form of qipmiq, qimmiq, etc., from the Proto Eskimo *qikmiʁ . Seward Peninsula Inupiaq dialects have qimugin or qimugun for 'dog,' parallel to Central Yupik qimuxta 'dog, lit. one that pulls.'"
—Lawrence Kaplan

I. July 2013
Dear J█,
I have your email address
from my good friend, Dr. K█n.
Given my writings
about the Island,
my name may be familiar to you.

I'm wondering how
your July trip
to the Island went.

Wish to be
of help to you,
if I can.

Blessings
and all best wishes,
Father L█ L. R█, S.J.

II. September 2014

And Hello
to you, dear Joan!
What a pleasant surprise
to receive
your echo
to my letter
to you
of some time ago!
I do sincerely
thank you for it.
I'm happy for you
that you had a chance
to go to the Island,
even if
for only a short time. As for the
"n███ c███ity dynamics
and ███ attacks"
I pretty
well know
what you are talking about.
Please, do not let them
bother you
any longer.

I'm sure they were
not meant to be all that
"personal,"
were triggered
in part by a certain
jealousy.
Let the past be past.
Dwell on the positive;
eliminate the negative.
I trust you know that the Little
Sisters have relocated
from Nome to Anchorage.
Talking with them
about matters of the Island
could be quite helpful to you.
Little Sister
A S
has kept me updated
on M S
and family.
M and M
were so good to me on that 1974 trip.
I guess M would be your aunt.
Greet your mother for me, please.
I have the fondest
memory of our time together
on the Island.

I took

many photos—

slides, black

and white

and color

prints. All

turned out well

and are accessible

in the archives

here,

as are also the Fr. Hubbard photos

and many others

of the Island,

as well as are much

other Island-related material.

In answer to your question:

I have no writing projects in work

at the present.

I continue to help

with the ██████████.

And I continue

to help out ████*s.*

"The church bell":

fate is mentioned

in the Alaskan Shepherd

article I wrote about the last

Masses on the

Island.

I guess that bell

and the statue of Christ

the King are the most

durable

human creations on the island.

If I might be of any help

to you

in any way,

dear J█,

feel most

free

to call on me.

God bless you,

your son█,

and all the dear

Islanders!

Father R█

III. January 1914

Your wife is dead,
and she died
just as she lived.
I told you
that God would punish her.
She lived bad,
she died bad,
and she was buried
like a dog.
And if you live bad,
you will die bad,
and also be buried
like a dog.
Father Bellarmine Lafortune, S.J.

Duck and Cover

the pale priest's teeth purple
as he milks dry a supply of altar wine
possessing less & less flour & oil

truth reduces to a worldview
survival reduces to truth

& if a polar bear moves across rough ice
& at three shots all clear
the future an age of disbelief
he, too, once lived on his mother's back
dark after dark

map before map & light before light
during drill after air raid drill
as he drills the children he teaches to cower
at three shots sounded into the air
extinguishing each kerosene lantern
lifting moss wicks from every seal oil lamp
draw gunnysacks animal hides & washboards
down over the glass panels of the small windows
of the square houses— now collapsed
& beneath— & now perhaps slumped into the sea
& land after land

Turning Back

I wished to be closer to my mother
to think of displacement in a different way.

To part the bright green new growth
of a plant she has asked me to gather.

We never imagined so many years apart.
I have no way to make amends.

Set adrift, I wanted to stay near the shore
of something familiar but instead I trace

the shape of *tuqqayuk*, sea lovage, wild
celery, with something other than my tongue.

I wish for my family to be its own refuge,
for the sorrow to become something islandic.

Someplace we can travel back to together
if we have to, if we make it through these days.

Epiphany

Scattered unproud in our conceit my firstborn child chalks
& anoints symbol & consecration at each door

of our newest new home while the new moon
sets in the west, & the winter sky

punctures the firmamental promise
it tarnishes, & tells me to be more rapt.

Earlier in the day someone I'd reminded
how I talk too much

sensed that I had more to say
& stood with me

on another threshold,
watching someone's

wife, disilluminated, walk away.
Another morning the cedars & pine

will take the north wind, having
juxtaposited one wife within one season of wives—

with the jaw of the phrasal
& with such unrelenting,

improvident weather.

With a Hammer & Drill-Bit to a Pane of Glass

I walk along a shore of salt and search for a sky
for a sky

reflecting blue
all winter

though a mirror
as it melts

won't show
what isn't there

& metal clapper
on metal &

a lost photograph
of the ouroboros

circling the bright
days in Poltava

& elsewhere as she
crouched astride

a latrine
where the eggs

where
(*Gogol's poppies?*)

inscribed with lines
could empty nothing

in supplication
to the erased

faces of the figures
carted everywhere

from the steppes
& another translator   in another translation

drunk with his many-
headed fire &

recalling the topple
and raze & afraid

of women armed
only with hand-turned

spoons, thatch, & our
children dreaming

of potency & releasing
all of us from poisons

& another day in Kharkiv
after the blizzarding

away, in the lobby
of a constructivist hotel

someone held Plath's poppies,
asked what if   it was what as if

they unblinded
& could make me see

After Anchorage II

irislike *the dark whorls* of Tammerkoski
tenterbellied *the rapids churn* sleep into my jetlag
nightmare *idioretinal* as my mother's husband hoses
a sprinkler's trickle against a wildfire *entangling drought*
down tributary valleys dense *with* tunneled spruce phloem
beetled of *sap.* Only in a bad dream would he have fought a sudden
blaze, *a sudden loss.*

The cops The halfway house The jail The hospital or The Troopers or something in 1984 or 1986 took both the parents of one of my cousins.
the goddess of the undertow
having too long gone unacknowledged
He lived with us until he used matches in the bottom bunk in the middle of the night to light a joint my mom rolled for her husband who had already gotten so high he could not hide it well enough. Something

caught fire, something we could extinguish. For years, though, my mom would wake to smoke after a few hours of sleep and then go back to bed. Once, her half-smoked cigarette fell from the ashtray still burning after she'd gone back to sleep. Who woke first but I, the child? On the leash? Who leapt over the fence to hang scabbling against the cedar, the peeling discount paint to *live*
to *break the fog*

Board of Game

you who did not expect
her to survive yet feared
she could set a trap
with metal jaws to snap

her neck below a grave
of snowdrop bulbs
black at the root
in black soil

in such darkness
we sought galantamine
to clear the mind
of a mother

to cleanse of guilt
for pain we cause one
still eyes turning
milkwhite with drifts

of ash of snow
settling on the brow
like a crown
of ache now

we cannot leave
children flushed
with green bittered
cloudberry knot

dwarf bramble beneath
cumuli peering up
upon those summits
all winter long to

rubus thicketing running
run over a crack
in the ice as it widens before
we could cross elsewhere

altogether else
where he trawls, he trawls

Board of Trade

He dreamed himself a pool of oil
& I his drowned wick
& wolf-like, he looked down on me.
Though my firstborn flew
as his first passenger,
& though later, when burning
me through a summer
of sad avarice, not once did my heart drop
as he pitched
one steep turn
after another—
I had come
to refuse my children close aboard
the boat of his
I myself would have never
let bear me,
the one he knew we could use to leave
& he feared used already, indifferent, working vanishment
from meaning
with the fury that to have chosen
implies choice.

The Angels of Yelling

I wasn't always this perfect.

On the drumlin burning
swords and munitions
will you waste?

Text me when you can be nice.

Resiliency exhausts:
don't want to metaphor anymore,
but drum, but map.

I don't know what you mean by that but don't really care to find out, either.

How do you process
& also help people hear
what you literally saw?

I don't think you should be allowed to date white people.

Plunder,
plunder,
plover.

It's not your kids' fault that their mother is an asshole.

The recollection

of such lost

abundance

It's no fucking secret that every man in your life is abusive.

a provocation,

a way to speak

to myself.

I'm sorry every man in your life is abusive, except me.

Nirruaqtuqtuŋa Ugiuvaŋmiuraaqtuaksrat

Harvested walrus sustain our line;
women-given atqit refrain our line.

Ava had lain tusks into the land:
morse takes mineral stain by our line.

Currents, rive always beneath the ice
we still beseech Sila in our line.

Child, and children of mine, always make
sure kiŋuġnit pertain to our line.

Uncle could regain his strength again
to visit together at shoreline.

You know Naviyuk (not J█ K█):
may such kinship remain in our line.

Qaggaa   Out There

navraaġniatuŋa   for old objects I search
navautaq.tuŋa   from sticks I make symbol signals for someone far away
we do undo & by now
things have long since
undergone repair . . .
piŋŋiq   red cedar from Siberia applied as harpoon handles
umiaqtatuq   s/he travels by skin boat
qanuġviġaqtuq   a way to find answers
qanuġvik   there comes into the open a way into a solution

& with Qisik   the youngest child of my uyuġu,
I go to Ugiuvak,   I go.
Called for my illua by those who have not unforgotten our dialect—
Qisik has chosen to transfigure
into an elder—a strong one—
with a mind that remembers everything,   even my oldest sister Awałuk, the one
all called by her nuniaq   & nicknamed Aakuaraq
Qisik remembers how   she always wanted
a daughter   but never had a daughter: she
bore only boys, including one, the last one,
who was born with teeth.
qugluiruaq   she greyed in a panic

Qisik remembers   how my oldest sister fumed so about
never producing a daughter   screeching at the spayed mutts some squatters
kept   always in and around her house.

my illua
one of the children of my assak, my father's sister. My sister J█████
would come under the name of her: Aġnauyaq. Years to the June day that
Qisik was conceived, the last of Qisik's milk teeth, a deciduous premolar,
came loose loosened

We have had dream-warm eyes.

umianik taŋmauruanik there stood skin boats on the coast
natiqituŋa I reached the shore ice
umianik taŋmauruanik there stood skin boats on the coast
umiqtuat taŋmaktut those traveling in skin boats came ashore

Malfunctions

Go ruin in the teeming
sea of the dead—
destroy, invert,
revert, revenge.

Count the uninoculated
birds all summer long
dropped lifelessly
from cloud to clod
and crest and crown
with clot and claw.

My jaw splits all morning with pain from
starlings I dreamt
I kicked across
some anabranch
of a weak god
whose riverine

banks I have scored
and crazed. From grease-
things, silver-winged,
thronged, empiercing
shame. Such nights I
have slept brux, doubled

against myself.

Ex Machina

rain sundering snow: the man-shaped hole in her brain
empties of hate as she combs a tangle of dark brown
hair from the crown of a child's head to whorl, blue
curl, & tendril :: the bruise beneath what's left of her
greening back into benignity & meanwhile the river
gurgles aleatoric into the harbor past an ukpeaġvik
as it gorges on the remains of a great blue heron
before the net catches her, until she is carried off
the tarmac, tagged & banded, released hours later:
not bird strike but another old danger, irruptive,
& much heavier in hand than an omen returned
from the combine of book machine & assignment,
a glib factory, compendium of forgetting. Different
different things have taught her respond not to brutality
with pettiness, & to set down the speculative weapons
she may have raised in a time of cultural distress.

Saakia

kamikłuk
mizu
siigriiq
marisiq

aglaaq
wassiq
tamałhuq
massaq
sassaq

taigun
kuupiaq
saaqalaq
sailaq

aglaan
miilaq
miisuk
suppun
kaamun

mukkaġun
taaŋa
qaqqiaŋuaq
saatkaaq

aglaktuŋa
nalikaaq
niaquŋusiun
saaqłaq
tiŋmiazun

Reclamation

<table>
<tr><td>loafer
soda-pop
cigarette
pill</td><td>barrel
coffee
sugar
sailor</td><td align="right">flour-sack
spirits
host
shotgun</td></tr>
<tr><td>something written</td><td>but; also</td><td align="right">i am writing</td></tr>
<tr><td>wristwatch
dollar
pottage
clock</td><td>soap
gunnysack
rifle
car</td><td align="right">trousers
aspirin
bar of chocolate
airplane</td></tr>
</table>

Letter from Austerlitz

Agate, ivory. Without
        alliance, I was told,
                we would not fill
                        the air with our difficult
                        musics. Always a mother,
                        & shame, & absent
                a worthwhile father. So I
came to know what it meant
to scratch *fragments are the only*
form he trusts onto the page—
suddenly I grew uncomfortable
to be loved, to know

                        what was wrong
                with the dream
was wrong with the people.

In Which The Poet Agrees That Being Alive Is a Whole Bunch of Being Wrong

& — yes— I confessed to a certain professionalism
when it came to pissing off men, to a handful of ash & more

intractable problems. Over-indulgence, at times,
                                        & yawn: increasingly tearful
& fearful for my well-
being, having stayed overlong twisting foxglove
& feverfew & ditigalis   (ambivalent shades I care both ways)
& parthenium—twee AF—meadowrue,
& rockcress toobeneath a grappling canopy of boreal
trees leafing out, perhaps always unleaving.
                        Allegedly, I no longer
had or have time for allusions
of the bitter sort. Sh█t is still
f██ed. The southside
of my contested yard suspired
with a combination of trills
given in a long string—
called a gallup of redpolls
when circumstances conspire
like that. Someone wrote,
"I am sorry to read
what's in the letter.
I hope things improve
for you." He, too, had
a friend named Rococo.

Being alone could have taken its toll.
A digression into Arendt
here, her gesture toward the "real
seductiveness of evil" & I, banal
as usual, mixed in with blokes
of commerce & state whose discursive
assertions sway "business is business"
& "war is war" into a beautiful
(if fading) inconsistency of the rhetorical
sort, & one in which we were all
enchanted by the consonance
of our own systems, values,
& vacuums. Sometimes I take on sh█t detail,

a perfunctory assignment: but of course,
that's where you'd find the dissolute
literati! Not Dover. Not days before one boards
the ferry from Abergwaun to Rosslare.

I'm supposed to get, at last, in this gray light,
to the "how" but still
I mire in the "why." Don't let's
forget the strand thick with earless seals
on its shifting banks. I was sometimes
not sorry, too.

The utility of my futile
testimony *something else*,
not a sum of its parts.

& here neither frog,
nor fovea, nor another other thing
other than mere principle

of subtraction, & nor a junction. At best,
somewhat badly signed— plausible
I gave consent to everlasting banishment.

After Anchorage III

I knew   of a woman

who
would not

debouch
her praise

into   a wire—

her firstborn
child,

synapses
bristling   with   torque,

whose fifth metacarpal

radiographed
again

and
over
again   now

gave sign of the

old,

healed

fracture,

whose

hands

refuse

to

lift

the

straight

-grain

stick

of

Pernambuco

to draw

across

chrome-wound

cold

strings

uncoiled

from

such

never,

shuts a door

against

her—

as some
vie
for coins,
coin

thudding
through fire
as
stones
lifted

from the

bellies
of
animals
culled as they moved north,

from the centers of stones
molten with envy,
magmatic,
like.

Saqtuliq

What could not be vulnerable in such changing
light? & what could anyone who has not
found a sense of the enormous
meaninglessness of
individuality
                    between the complex anticipation of the sea
as it parallels the voluble insinuations of the river
            thick with rich fish flush with eggs
begin to understand
that to lose one's land
has nothing to do with storms?

Submerged willow brush & a wolverine,
& a mother, or a woman who would be one:
she sees the others who will set to work,

turning the bureaucracy of such vulgar tongues
as driftwood serries into the flaw

of her throat, larger in circumference
than the loss I will no longer
measure palm by palm.

Counterpoem

Ordering myself to announce what I knew of love
I could only recall the sky as it darkened,
a cache of reindeer exposed as the ice
lens that made their grave thawed.
Looking for another island
                    without awareness
that the islet had long since
          lost me   unlike the man
                    who may have
                              knocked
baleen inlay loose
from ivory, an admonition or an accident.

I will wait for him to walk the trail
with me though the trail
                         today fills with rain, hail. More rain.
We both know little, only that we will find
a way through deluge, remembering
something else of love: that the sky will change
with abandon, with radiant syncope.

Elixirs for Words to Come

The first thing I will do: make
myself indecipherable
to you, for

our understanding
revises a kind of hunger.

My language has taken on
all manner of smog. I
come to fear:

I come to fear the things
that inspire me

in the wake
of our destroyers.

I dream of my dead
peers. I see how they do
not want pretty

things. I know they do
not want me to describe pain

of any kind. They gesture
to the gold dredges
hinging into the earth,

they sink down
as gelisol thaws,

as we all slink
down into a kind
of hell.

Let us wash ourselves in those waters.
Let us thirst because we cannot drink them.
Let our mothers tell us of their girlhoods:

the ones they lost when they rolled willow
leaves tight in toilet paper:
smoked not to get high, not to die,

but only to see visions of Mary,
that Mary, who was some kind
of mother.

Unfinishing

women with hair the color of tar
women with debt irrefutable

women with eyes darker than broth
thickened by pulverized nettle

women like these remind women—
green seeds sprout from black snow

after eruption   after ash—
like glass that cuts the lungs

when every year proves
itself to land disaster

women like me learn
how to make our flaws

iridescent as gutter oil
sheening in runoff

shining beneath linden trees
cognomens for our shared end

No Litanies, No

strangers here.
No more aching for the useful goods I left behind.
No more uncles left to come to me in times of need.
No more boy cousins to give me what they think could reach
me, wound me. They age into men and petrify. They turn to shadow,
night terror, sacks of lant, or jurisdictional abstraction. No
spouse. No breach. No home left to long for.

No more *I want to go home.* No more *I want to go into another time.*
No more want, just need. Nothing real.
No ease of pain. No east left to get, to escape.
No more knives carried past as if by pure silver rivers.
Just hunger. Hunger for the oil I could render from a seal.
Not the one another turns only into a symbol, an arcanity.

Yes

I once was the baby
who was given brackish water
in a rubber-nippled bottle,
a baby squalling for days
as my kidneys faltered.
Yes it was death
that groped for me then.

Yes:

into the same lagoon some decades later
my father's recklessness sent him and one of the men
he first most wished for me to marry.

Yes, my father told me he should have left my mother before I helled into his world.
Yes, for once, he was right.

Counterpoem I

of the long and disorienting strokes,
she told me how distant they drew her from herself,

later how she held an image of me in the snow
smoking on the upper west side.

Never spoke of the dogcatching man who sold
his community role.

I could have spent so
many hours listening to her

instead of passing the time since in these wounds,
collecting ash, wondering how the wind bore

white petals to gather in my shadow,
as small as I make me. She said

she loved that image of me. I disclose
to her how I think someone has killed

the generator, how the task of writing goes
on with the faithful against the war.

After Anchorage IV

of gadolinium, November-veined, copper on the tongue
        & summoning sleep & ether though wide-awake
after click & whir & click again of excision & extraction

& artery notched & every hand in the dim back room
        summoned to press the bloodied breast to bone
& told to *find calm* & *stay calm* & O type O negative

& *calm* & *fuck* & the radiologist who would remember
        the day years after, bumbling, mutters
& with whiskey-thick fingers on black Friday & routine

gone awry & no luck for transfusion & hours later
        to be wheeled out into the familiar lobby to my
children's father & my mother's husband who, terse

& ever inconvenienced by my systems of synapse & pulse,

would warn me off from flying the next day & the next
        through Seattle & de Gaulle & landing bleary at Boryspil
& to blur through birch woods, woozy still, & sore

& o sour viburnum opulus & o ash & ache to come

First

We both know who believed snow, who denied it,
when you finally came to walk me to the river.

I forget I am not pure, how little
that part of the story ever matters.

What matters, maybe—how long
I have been waiting, and with such

impatience. At the end I think I will know
what pure means, what I meant to insist back

into my blood, whatever it meant to want
to live. Whatever inevitable ruin.

Already, for some years, my head has grown
heavy and my ear bent towards another

across our difficult and shared country, so.
Whatever it means, I'm not yours.

A Thousand Signs

Let's say little of what faith
        fled in the old year
betwixt the wrong Hanover
        & rise of Swiss wisteria
through a bellrung Ascension-day
        after screenings of *Imajuik* & *Lena*
River & *Three Thousand* & before our
        most unexecuted family
snapshot afront Schrödinger's cat

        between the drawn-out
dawn   noontide   dusk
        of the mostly-silent faraway
fjords during the warm weeks
        when they offered up such
green asaaqłuk & tugaayuk
        for me to glean
fresh with new astonishment
        for those whose sung
songs turn to the living
        with the dead

for those whose songs turn
        from fleece & nickel
to owl & bone

before traveling through Oslo
& Reykjavík to draw
& drink bright clear
water with my son
from the springs at the feet
of Singatook as he towered
over the last of us
amidst the willows   arnica   frigid
shooting stars   avens   & moss
campion before I even left for Ohio
& even more so when I got there

& later along the ridge
where I often hear
the wolves before I see them
I chewed a grasp
of crakeberry yarrow
&   labrador tea leaves
in case a sodden August
could not douse the perils
of late-season burns
but before I called
& emailed SeaWorld
to report a tangled sea
lion pup while I let the syntax

of the past begin to leave me
then when with my mother's
husband stirring at the first
light in November to see thin
hours heft the shadows
of the Chugach through tall grasses
as they paled threatening a dark

season & I coughed some arsenic
or cadmium dust from my lungs
with a poet whose *Two*

Signatures had begun
to walk me back into my line & ran
late to gather Oleksandra

between Kyiv & Munich & Minneapolis
& Seattle & Portland & Minneapolis
& Munich & Kyiv & though we might

have rolled our eyes
during renditions suffering
from too much unearned ease

met first to posit & then to prove
        that diffidence probably causes
the demotic conditions
        under which we live—
which is to point out only in this poem
        the white hyacinth I forced
on the coffee table into bloom with
        sweetness near unbearable
as a companion to my drowsing

        a dream before our mutual
going brown   a kind
        of drowning   a kind
of gladness to stray
        so far away
from Boston, for
        having made it
into bed alone
        by default, not pathology—

as if some ardent flash and ash
        and sudden terseness
could just appear
        and go ignored. As if nothing
ever happened, as if
        I could still make
a poem from
        something so simple.

Deteriorating from a lack
        of mischief a little sooner
than planned, I find, latish: in order
        to yearn, I could type some words
and then erase them. As if

        I have fooled anyone, much less
the children, into thinking
        of forgetting such agitation
in my tone with: *This poem*
        is bad, isn't it? I could
promise to start
        a fire later, ask
if we might again
        take up the tools.

Obtaining the necessary language, one
    of my children reminds me
that we continue to grow things here
    where nothing fallows. Possible
here to step out back and hear the golden-
    crowned kinglet, dark-eyed junco,
red-breasted nuthatch, song
    sparrow, Anna's hummingbird.

"I don't know,
    I'm not listening"
makes its way into a poem
    easier than anything else,
though the reply, in full, may souse
    my second, half-earned life:
"I don't know, I'm not listening to it."

In Which the Poems and Poets Agree That They Are the Result of Choices They Have Made Along the Way

The silver of the lake caught
in the net, like a provocation.

The translation under the writing —
How long have you been running?

I tried to answer, am still trying. A poem,
too, holds secrets that it cannot tell.

Gone septic from a spider bite, the anger
only troubles like sorrow until it goes away.

You wish you were home? Yes. But —
mitiktuq — it came unraveled.

I used to think I preferred to dream
with a man only after he bedded me

and then there are the real poems
where the language creates its own tension.

Where the language reminds us
to create a story and to become part of it,

to stay alive until we come back.

After Anchorage V

suppose a bluescoured sky

though I found no hook, no
anchor, nothing to hold me—

& wrote
from the bright, cold spring
& there he led us in circles

in a box
in a city
in a high-storied hold

opposed

I became nothing more
than something to storm
scale & then subtract

O
to have been the penultimate she let
she left—isthmic—to be hewn to rock
or something visible to all

Without Anchorage

We practice dreaming into the future, steeping the leaves of Labrador tea we now grow in a broad pot on a patio, grind rice through until glutinous, harvest the tops of the nodding onions flash-frozen with approximate winter's sudden onset, haul the tenderest medicines inside losing only the laurel: hyssop, arnica, basketgrass sagrit seem, so far, well-suited to survive this overdue bitterness. The moon— of course the moon —gleams its crescent through the fine ice suspended in the refracting atmosphere of our newest west.

On the last days of the last year we ferried black plastic bins from my childhood bedroom closet (that adults once used to cultivate homegrown weed even though the violet blare of the grow light made it hard to fall asleep) to the Anchorage airport post office, a double sundog haloing the dim sun whose incandescence still has not sloughed the dark season's fractal hoarfrost from the trees.

We bought too many boxes to hold the storage bins' contents: journals of mine read and reread by others over four decades, photographs and negatives from my life apparently misspent. Strapping tape gave up its adhesion to the bonesnapping cold. One box last week arrived rent so deep that we can only imagine what must have been lost in transit.

Outcast together again in this new year. In the old one a family consisted of two grandparents, one mother and two children. Now, my child, I agree that I may have finally disobeyed my mother, who scolded my pregnancy: "it better not be a girl." Perplexed, recalling her tenderness when she plaited my waistlength hair for eleven years, the glee with which she accoutered me in jelly shoes, metal earrings, jeweltoned dresses, I'd asked, "mom, I thought I was pretty good for a girl. I didn't taaŋaq until I was out from under your roof?"

Stern, shhe replied: "You've never disobeyed me before, you won't start now." Not me, then, who disobeys *her* when I drop you off at school and you hand me a note that tells me on the folded front not to read it until I've dropped your brother off at school.

I open it at a red light while he stares vatic into his phone. Within, you address me: *mother*, you tell me ████████, what you would like ████████. Not you who disobeys. We live through our names. We survive only through changing.

Before 12 I was disowned, abandoned, ignored, spanked, and struck, with bars of Irish Spring shoved into my mouth each time I refused to let such punishments take. As an adult I once barricaded my bedroom door against the rage of my mother's husband with a couch. He punched through the door at eye level to see me trapped inside, crying. His brother with my mother in the front of the house, unsurprised by this violence.

At the end of the old year, his wife ████████████████████, her daughter somehow still ████████████████████, the woman's husband disowns again. I disobey my mother (whose hair I brush, whose dentures I disinfect

overnight, whose CPAP machine I fill with distilled water, whose
grandchildren I bring from east and south,
whose anaq I wipe when I lift her from the toilet remembering how he broke
her tailbone trying to kick a pregnancy out of her before we barricaded
ourselves in a childhood home's only bathroom while we waited

for the police to arrive and arrest him hours after she delivered a baby girl
dead into the commode bowl while I held her knees and tried not to watch
her bleed)
whose eyes I clear of crust and clog, whose bed I make each night when
visiting hours end. His meant-to-harrow split. We leave her, traveling south.
With us flurrying snow freezes on the asphalt.
Weeks of ice, of rain, of ice, will follow

and I recall the time I trailed off into myself:
"I come from a long line of Inuit . . ."
Remembering your retort:
"well, then, since you made me, I come from an even longer line."

Infinitive

There is nothing sentimental
in this forest. A squall, birch
boughs sibilant. Some hearth
upwind glut with wet wood.

You, taken with a fine polish,
should have wed the woman
you would have loved: nothing
in this forest. Sentimental,

I dwelt once beneath a linden tree
sprung up between leaves of mica,
scaffolds, lanes of passing traffic.
Its redolence stifling and flawless,

conditional. I do not miss it.
Torn from a tangled understory
underfoot, a scud of clubmoss
spores blown burns rapid, right.

On No Longer Being a Carbon-Offset Girlfriend

Inscribing invisible language
new with mar and garble I archive
nothing but atmosphere—

such music is dry and sharp
and all the darkness I have grasped
grows legible,

nothing like rivers of young ice
dazzling blue-white. Once
such glut confusion

could bruise by every weapon or want
as cold tongues turned the land
for life, as they

mixed the rich
into the soil
to raise one last forest

for cambium to gargle
and soothe a girl
into something domestic.

To consume to extinction,
to leer at hairgrass
as it too loses

its scale. If I had never ceded
continents, how could
I usher another

diminishment? Another gesture
of change or repair
in a dew-world

wet with gold or granite,
of carved earth
thick with saplings

and the heal of fireweed
and sorrel
rising from silted earth

churned by a composed,
deliberate might? Compulsion
thrives in a grid-girded skull,

anarchic on its ruined face.
What parsimony yet smothers
and bakes me as I erase

cities, submerge countries, drowning
the engines and braying machines
of empire? My gristle nothing

but abundance, my inner
rind familiar and serviceable
as they skinned

my throat to make me bleed. As I
funnel gas into a skiff
as if—as if at sea.

Patiq

Pulaumaruŋa ⊗. Piŋigiiga.
Niġiksranik payukia ⊗.
Kavusruŋa. Puġiktuq. Piŋilsraiga.

Tununami nauŋ tiŋmiaqłania.vaura.tuq?

Inipika.tuq. Kaŋŋigiga:
Pitaialaq. Sutailaq.
Nunataitmiuq uvva.

Atagumuq imma:

kigrawik, kayuqtuq, nunivaaksrat,
pamiuqtaq, paułuk, piġaluyak,
aliuġaq, quzimaq, piknik,

mazu, kavlaq, aukpalitiŋiq,
suġat, suak, milugataq,
kimagluk, quŋuliq, paitqsinaaq ::

izauġaitka

quvliliruŋa

uyayula

Marrow

I am visiting ⊗ I fear for her safety.
To ⊗ I brought nourishment.
I traveled through a wave in rough seas. She is trenchant. I fear for her.

Remember how there used to be many birds at the back of the island?

There is an image that has been reflected. I reached the end of it, my limit, my destination:
all is depleted. There is nothing left.
No land to be seen anywhere.

Listen to that distant sound:

peregrine falcon, red fox, berries and greens growing to profusion from the profuse earth,
fireweed, cormorant, compressed freshwater ice which is blue in hue,
sorrel, wild rhubarb, tall cottongrass,

wild potato, black bearberry, red phalarope,
blueberries, fish roe, coltsfoot,
bitter sourdock, sourgrass, woolly lousewort ::

gather them

my eyes are brimming with tears: I

whirlwind

On Purpose

I could let one near and part
the months ahead with music,
with caraway loaves, with sprats
as they glint from their tin
while the tap runs clear.

Maybe no one will near
and tear the threat—latent,
invasive—of the
Asperula odorata
I transearthed last summer

with topsoil into moss
and rock on the east slope's
shade beneath the choreographic
sprawl of these Japanese maples.
Maybe, dear, the harlequin

glorybower will survive to flower
white again then the pink calyces
will fall away and refuse to drop
the metallic bright blue
drupes like griefs

misplaced from another
yesterday story and maybe all
this time I would never
have needed
the indispensable

fifth to restore me. Maybe
I'll take to the sensible
note, will keep my hands full
cradling my own
head, maybe

the spring will
come, you'll fly off
to Kaohsiung,
maybe leaving room
for someone

to climb into my life
despite the brambles,
maybe for them.

Milugataq Tumait

kiŋuliq aviġlamiaq ugiumi unnuatuq
uvaġna.tuq apsruq aviruq avigaa
ikparak unnugaa mazaq taaqsiruk

agnaq sakłaruq igliayaaqtuq uivraaqtuq sigunun
aukaa Aaŋaayuliqti iġmit ipqaziruq
massam siġniga sawiviniq sawisrkhaq

tigluuraq sallitik itisaq taaqtut
uaqtuq tammairuq ikparaaq ugiuq

igliayaaqtuq
Báhpajávri: Prestvannet nani
(atali'aa) tatigzraq tiŋmiġruat
nauyuait tuułit sitamat

katumarut. Tiġitkuatyat
uglut nivaalarut
malikataġaa naniq
nuna mazaġaa: nausiat quqsatuaq
quvlatut

Mapkutitaaġruaq Tumitchiat

aaqtuaq

salumaruq kaivaluktaa killiŋiqsit-
savił̣ġaq qivligguiñ savił̣haq

tigluuraġa saṭiluŋ una itiniq
aġili tammaiṭi ukiutqik

kiavaluisaaqtuaq
Báhpajávri: Prestvannet *nani*
(atiruakavsak) tatigrak tulukaat
nauyat tuułit sisamat

kasimaniq mitqutaḷaq
ugluutit nipaturut
malliutigaa
uvlumi: nauriat quqsuqtaaq
qunmuktut

milugataq unnuaġuq
aliugaq qizuksitut ~~iguit~~

kaġnaqtaat kiŋuġ,liġiit aaġlatuq
taqqiq naaġatuq puġiilaq
tiimiaqruq palligrat

qivirat kaumaaġviktuŋa taqmaq
salliuruq quŋŋuq

naġituq riiġutit
taamnaguuqaaŋ maani

aggiriruq
auk kiniqtuaq

qayuq qaġitaq uaġiaġaa
kuiġaa silaavyiun
uuna.tuq nulluairuq quvisuŋaq.

aaka iglua agvuaa savviraqtuq
atali milugataq aataq/
paatitaaq misataaq

sura [. . .] sigu nunivakaksrat
izaġulik/ikuusuuk pamiuqtaq
sura/agraga quaqsaaqtut

mapkutitaaġtuaq unnuġruaq
aliugani nutchuktaat ~~akutuqpalitik~~

siaktuat uiguligiit aġluqtuaq
imigluktittuq kinnauruq
pakiksimaruaq palliŋit

qipitaq igvik aiñiġmiutaqtuaq imnaliq
salliq iḷuvvik

qaiqsaġaa taiguat
suviksraiqsuq maani

aggisuutiraa
auk kiniqtuaq

qayuq qaqisalik puvlaksiaq
kuviqsaa siḷaavyiun
uunaqtuq nullakaa maniuraq

una aaka aippaq sisamautaq saviŋmi
milukataqliaq aiñaq/
paatitaaq palauvaksraġiitchuaq

siqupayaaqtuq akutuqpalik agmaqtuaq
isaġulik/ikuusuich quppiqutaq
sura/quaqsaaqtuŋa

qaqqiaq iġalugvik igalugruaq
aġagriq qatik aġagriq qayuq aġiaguq

suranik taŋiqłuuŋa
qunŋiq (kanaakituuraq)
tapłigait qayuq ayauŋuaq

kawiqtuaq (atali'aa kikmik)
nanuiyun
immuksiiq mizu
puivraa

aqpik aqpik
aukpaluaqsruq aukpaluaqiruq
saayu suġat immiuqtuq

nagaun aguġluuraq
nikisrat iluaqsiruq
mamisiami nagusituŋa

aulaġiruq qigiqtaq
qigiqtaqpauraq
saġurut/tiliuq[-]

aulaiqtut waisiq

SASSAQ

punniq aŋayuqsraq igalugruaq
qargiq /aqargiq puviachiaq
uqsruutilik iŋaluatchiat

uqpik
piagniq qunŋiq
tavliktuq imiġaq argaġñaq/avaatchiqiq

kaviqsaaq (uqpiŋñaqtunqayaq)
nanuktaaġun
immuk (/autchiivik/ayauiḷaq) usiġaqtuġniq
puuvruqtuq

aqpik aqpik
aqpik aqpik kaviġtuaq
saiyu asiaviqutaq iksiaksraq

nuvulu avḷuqtaun
sayyaglaŋa sayakturuŋa
sayyaglaŋa sayakturuŋa niġipkaqavsi

aullaqtuq qikitaq tapqaq
tapqaqaġuuruq
aŋalvuk/saqquqtut/tilliñ siqiñuraq

qasuqtut qasulit nutqaqtit takituaq

~~qiniŋilatiut tigurigaluġnatiŋ.~~

Acknowledgments

Grateful acknowledgement is made to the editors of the following publications, who first published versions of these poems:

Academy of American Poets, Arctic and Circumpolar Indigenous Futurisms, Bare Life Review, Duck Quarterly, Harvard University Press, High Country News, Kenyon Review, Land Without: Arctic and Circumpolar Indigenous Futurisms, Orion, Poetry, Poetry Daily, Shō, Staircase Books, Stronger Together: Bering Strait Communities Respond to the COVID-19 Pandemic, Territory, The Third Thing Press, Under A Warm Green Linden, and *Water~Stone Review.*